INDOOR and OUTDOOR GAMES

Neeru Vajpai

RED TURTLE
RUPA

Published in Red Turtle by
Rupa Publications India Pvt. Ltd 2017
7/16, Ansari Road, Daryaganj
New Delhi 110002

Sales centres:
Allahabad Bengaluru Chennai
Hyderabad Jaipur Kathmandu
Kolkata Mumbai

Text Copyright © Neeru Vajpai 2017
Illustrations Copyright © Rupa Publications India Pvt. Ltd 2017
Design by Roy Creation

The views and opinions expressed in this book are the author's own and the facts are as reported by him/her which have been verified to the extent possible, and the publishers are not in any way liable for the same.

ISBN: 978-81-291-4633-5

First impression 2017

10 9 8 7 6 5 4 3 2 1

The moral right of the author has been asserted.

This book belongs to:

....

....

Games are fun! Games help you to keep fit, allow you to communicate with others and work together with your friends. The more friends you have to play games, the merrier it is! Running about and playing outdoors is the best activity.

But what would you do on a rainy day, a cold day or a really hot day when you cannot step outside to play? Well, there are some games that you can play indoors, and have as much fun. Let us find out how to play these games. Let's begin!

INDOOR GAMES

Colour My World

This is something that lets you use your creativity. You can do this either alone or with your friends.

You will need:

- Half a chart paper (for each player)
- Watercolours
- Plastic tray
- Half an onion
- Half a ladyfinger, onion or capsicum

Place the watercolours on a plastic tray. Now take the chart paper. Take the piece of onion or ladyfinger, dip it in a watercolour and stamp it on the chart paper. Create your own designs using them. You can even draw a pattern first and fill colours in it using the vegetables.

Each player creates his or her own design. Once complete, you can put up your artwork on your bedroom wall.

Paper and Trinkets Collage

This activity also brings out your creativity.

You will need:

- Paper
- Glue
- Coloured paper cut into small strips, triangles and circles.
- Small trinkets like old buttons, sequins, googly eyes, beads etc

Draw what you like. It can be anything from a house to an elephant.

Take out some glue on a plate.

Put glue on the coloured paper cuttings and small trinkets. Place these glued items one by one onto your drawing. Let the glue dry. Your work of art is now for everyone to see.

Bowl-a-Rama

Create your own bowling alley. A minimum of 2 players can play this game.

You will need:

- 6–10 empty plastic bottles
- A small ball
- Water

Take 6–10 empty bottles. Half fill these with water or sand to prevent them from falling easily.

Each player will get three chances to strike the bottles with the ball. If a player is able to make all the bottles fall down at the first go, he or she is a clear winner. If this does not happen, the player has two more chances to do so. At the end of a player's turn, count the number of bottles that are left standing.

The second player will now attempt to topple the bottles. You need to record the number of bottles left standing.

Decide on the number of sets for each player to play. When the game ends, count the number of bottles that were left standing at the end of each set for every player.

The player who had the least number of bottles standing is the winner.

Tic-tac-toe

You will only need one of your friends to play this game.

You will need:

- A paper and a pencil

Draw two small lines horizontally and two lines vertically crossing them. This is how it will look.

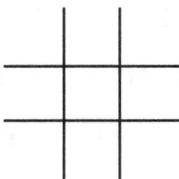

You will be player 'x' and your friend will be player 'o'. You will begin by marking 'x' anywhere in the grid. Then your friend will place an 'o' in the grid.

This game will end only when either of you has got either 'x' or 'o' in a straight line or diagonally inside the grid. The player who does this first is the winner.

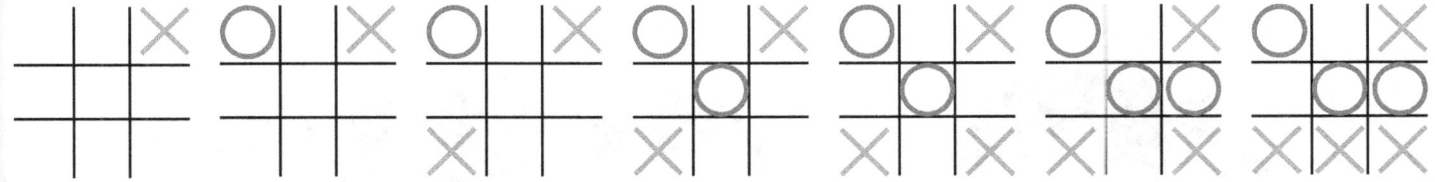

Look at the set of pictures arranged sequentially above. These will help you to understand how to win the game. In the above sequence, the player 'o' would have won if player 'x' had not put a cross diagonally below 'o'.

This game will make you sharper and improve your observation skills.

Simon Says

You can play this game with three or more of your friends. It will be more fun if there are more players. This game can be played indoors as well as outdoors.

You and your friends will choose who will be 'Simon'. He/she will stand before the other players. The player who becomes 'Simon' will issue instructions in this manner: "Simon says, put your hands up". Each of the players will have to follow the instructions of 'Simon' instantly. If a player cannot follow Simon, he/she is out of the game. Sometimes, Simon can also give incomplete instructions like "clap your hands" without saying, "Simon says". If a player follows this instruction, he/she is out of the game as well.

Simon has to get every player out as quickly as possible. The last player who remains after all others are out is the winner. He/she will become the next Simon. It is important to remain attentive during this game.

Rock-Paper-Scissors

This is a game played with hand movements. You can play this game with many friends. One of you can keep the score.

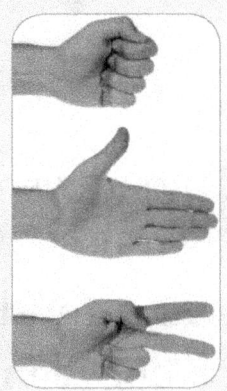  

You have to form one of the three shapes shown with your hand. A simple fist is the 'rock'; open palm is the 'paper' and a fist with the middle and index fingers forming a 'v' is 'scissors'.

In order to begin the game, say aloud, "rock-paper-scissors", raise one hand and throw it forward in one of the three shapes before the other players. The other players will need to do so at the same time. For e.g. if player 1 decides to play 'scissors', then player 2 will beat him/her who has chosen 'rock' because 'rock crushes scissors'. If player 1 chooses 'paper', player 2 will lose because 'paper covers the rock'.

If player 1 chooses 'paper' and the other chooses 'scissors' then 'paper' would lose as 'scissors cuts paper'.

Let us put it simply:

1.   Rock + scissors = rock is the winner
2.   Rock + paper = paper is the winner
3.   Paper + scissors = scissors is the winner

If the players choose the same shape, the game is a tie. The game will continue until there is a winner. The players need to be quick and guess what the other would choose in order to win.

Don't Step on the Lava

In this game you have to imagine that the floor is made of lava. There are safe spots across the room. The aim of the game is to cross the lava without touching the floor.

You will need:

- A4 sized coloured paper sheets or pages of old newspapers and a two-sided sticky tape or sellotape.

First, stick the coloured papers across the floor in a random manner making a sort of bridge. There should be gaps between the papers. Decide which is the safe spot across the room.

Now imagine that the floor is made of lava. The sheets of paper are your only means to go safely across the lava. The players need to keep moving from one paper to the other. The moment a player shouts, 'The floor is lava!' the game begins. All the players must step on the sheets and attempt to go across to the place of safety. Any player who steps on the floor is out of the game. The player who first reaches the point of safety has won.

Lion's Cub

This game is a great means of amusement if there are many players.

You will need:

• A small stuffed toy

Choose among yourselves a player who will be the 'lion'. The lion will sit facing the wall and with its back towards the other players. He/she must sit at least ten feet away from other players. The stuffed toy is kept behind the lion who pretends that it is its cub.

The remaining players will take turns to come up silently behind the lion to steal its cub. If the lion hears the players sneaking behind him, he will roar and turn around.

If he catches the player, he/she will become the new lion. The first lion will then join the other players. If there is no one near when the lion roars, then he/she continues to be the lion.

Duck, Duck, Goose

You can play this game both indoors and outdoors. A minimum of six players are needed to play this game.

All the players should sit down in a big circle. One among them will remain standing. He/she will be called 'It'. The game begins when 'It' goes around the circle calling out 'duck' while touching each player. While going around the circle, 'It' will suddenly say 'goose' and touch someone. As soon as someone is goose, he/she has to get up and chase 'It' around the circle to get back to his/her seat.

If the player who is goose is unable to reach his/her place before 'It' reaches there, the goose becomes 'It'. In this manner, the game will go on.

Chinese Whisper

This game is most enjoyed with a large group of players.

All the players will sit in a circle or stand in a line. A player will think of a short message and whisper it into the ear of the player next to him/her. Repeat message softly so that the others are unable to hear it. In this manner, the message will be whispered from player to player till it reaches the last person.

The last player will now say the message aloud instead of whispering. Guess what! You will realise that this was not the message you had whispered at the beginning! The original message changed to something else because everybody heard something different!

This game teaches you to modulate your voice and listen attentively to others.

Doggy, Where's Your Bone?

You will need at least six players to play this game.

A child will play the part of a dog. The dog will sit on a chair with his/her eyes closed and with his back towards other players. A small object like an eraser, a paper clip or a coin is placed below the dog's chair. This object is called the bone. When everything is in place, all the players except the dog will sing:

"Doggy, doggy, where's your bone?
Somebody stole it from your home."

While the players are singing, one among them will sneak up quietly, steal the bone and go back to his/her place. Then, everyone will sing:

"Doggy, doggy, where's your bone?
Somebody stole it from your home.
Guess who it might be?"

Sometimes, the bone is not stolen though the players change the song.

The player pretending to be dog will now turn around and open his/her eyes. He/she gets three chances to guess who has taken the bone. All the players should put their hands behind their backs pretending that they have the bone.

If guessed correctly, then the person who has the bone becomes the dog. Otherwise, he/she will continue to be the dog. This game will teach you how to guess by reading the expressions on the faces of your playmates.

OUTDOOR GAMES

I am sure your mother would love you to be active and get some fresh air as well. Outdoor games are a good way for you to stay healthy as they provide good exercise. Won't it be fun to learn to play some outdoor games!

Tag

This is an enjoyable game and can even be played with a few players. Of course, it is more fun when there are more children. It is best played in a park or garden as you would need to run.

One child will be 'It'. 'It' will now chase the other players, trying to touch anyone, while everybody runs away. All the players will run around 'It', trying to dodge him/her so that they cannot be touched. The moment 'It' touches a player, he/she will now become 'It' and the game will start again.

Tag is a good running exercise and it also teaches you how to dodge.

Cross Tag

This game is played in the same manner as Tag.

In this game, if any player crosses or runs between 'It' and the person whom 'It' is chasing, then 'It' will start chasing that player instead of the former, and try to tag him/her.

Chain Tag

This game is a variation of Tag too. The rules remain the same as those of Tag. Here, when 'It' catches a player, he/she will joins hands with 'It' to catch others.

When either of the two chasers touch another player, he/she too will join hands with them, forming a chain. In this manner, the game will go on until all the players are caught. Sometimes when there are too many children playing, the chain can be split into two.

The player who was caught first becomes the next 'It'. The last player who has not been caught is the winner of the game.

Lock and Key

This game is another fun variation of Tag. A minimum of five players can play this game. One of the players will be chosen as 'It'. 'It' will run around to catch the other players.

When 'It' catches a player, 'It' will shout "LOCK". This means that the player caught is 'locked' and cannot move. In similar manner, 'It' has to lock everyone in the game.

Other players who are running about can touch the "locked" player and shout "KEY". The locked player can now run around once more. If 'It' gets all of you locked, he/she wins. The first player caught will become the next 'It'.

Dog and the Bone

Divide yourselves into two teams. One player will become the Leader. He/she will divide the players into two teams and number both teams from 1 to 10.

Both teams will stand in two lines facing each other, keeping a few feet of distance between them. Keep the bone (any stuffed toy or handkerchief) in the middle of the playing area.

The Leader will stand where the bone is and call out a number. Then, the player from each team with that number will come forward and try to grab the bone and run back to their own team.

If a player of Team A picks up the bone and runs, the player of the other team will try to prevent him/her from taking the bone to his/her team. The team that manages to bring the bone safely home maximum number of times wins the game.

Red Light, Green Light

In this game, one of the players becomes the Stoplight.

The other players will stand in a line about five metres away from the Stoplight.

When everyone is ready, the Stoplight turns his/her back to the players and calls out 'green light'. At once, all the players will start moving towards Stoplight. Their aim is to try and touch Stoplight.

The Stoplight can say 'red light' at any time and turn around. This means that all the players should stop moving. If a player is caught moving, he/she is out.

The game will start again when Stoplight turns his/her back and says 'green light'. The first one to touch the Stoplight wins the game and will become the Stoplight in the next game. If Stoplight is able to get all the children out before they are able to touch him/her, the Stoplight wins.

Hide and Seek

This is a very popular game. You can play it indoors also. Before you start playing, assign a boundary, so that no one hides beyond that place. A tree or a wall can be used as the 'base'. Select one of the players to be the Seeker. The Seeker will close his eyes and count till fifty loudly so that everyone can hear him. The rest of the players must hide themselves within that time. Once the Seeker has finished counting, he/she will turn around and shout: "Coming". The Seeker has to look and find each of the players. The moment the Seeker sees someone, he/she has to shout: "I spy" and call out the name of that person. The player who has been caught first will be the next Seeker and the one caught last will win the game. If any player touches the home base or touches the Seeker from behind, the Seeker will continue to be the Seeker in the next game too.

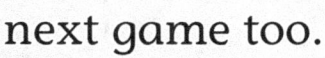

London Statue

London Statue is a variation of the game Red Light, Green Light. A player will be chosen as 'It'. 'It' will stand before the other players and turn his/her back.

'It' will spell out "L.O.N.D.O.N Statue" either very slowly or very quickly when his/her back is turned. All the players will move while 'It' is calling out "London".

The moment 'It' says 'Statue', the players will have to stop moving. They have to stand absolutely still. When the players are Statue, 'It' can crack jokes, talk or ask questions trying to make the players laugh or move. If 'It' catches anyone moving, he/she is out of the game. The game continues in this manner until someone is able to touch 'It' or all the players are caught moving by 'It' and he/she has won.

Wolf's Dinner Time

This game is best played in a big group.

One of the players becomes the Wolf. The Wolf stands with his/her back to the other players. The other players will stand about fifteen feet away from the Wolf. When standing thus, the players will call out, "What is the time, Mr Wolf?"

The Wolf will turn around and reply e.g. "3 o'clock".

The players will then take three steps forward.

The game will continue in this manner till all the players are standing quite close to the Wolf. Now, when the players call out, "What is the time, Mr Wolf?", the Wolf will turn around and reply, "Dinner time". The Wolf will then start chasing the players as they rush back to the start line.

If the Wolf catches a player before he/she has reached the start line, that player will become the Wolf. If the Wolf is unable to catch anyone, the next game will begin with the same Wolf.

Red Letter

A minimum of four or five players are needed for this game.

One among the players becomes the Leader and stands with his/her back to the others. The other players will stand about ten to fifteen metres away from the Leader.

The Leader begins the game by calling out any letter of the alphabet, for example, 'A'.

The players whose names have the letter 'A', will move forward. If a player's name contains the letter twice, he/she will move forward by taking two steps. Similarly, if a name has the letter thrice, that player takes three steps.

The Leader will continue to call out letters of the alphabet until someone reaches the Leader, taps him/her and runs back. If the Leader manages to catch this player, then he/she is out of the game. In this manner, the Leader has to get all players out. The first player caught will become the next Leader.

Tippy Tippy Tap

You will enjoy playing this game in the garden when the flowers are in full bloom. There should be at least six players to play this game. One of the players will be 'It' and stand at a distance. The other players will start the game saying, "Tippy tippy tap, what colour do you want?"

'It' will then name a colour, "I want red colour."

The moment 'It' has said a colour, all the players will run to find things of that colour and touch it. The colour could be on your clothes, any flower or any object. All this while, 'It' will chase the players as they find the colour. Any player who is unable to find the colour and is caught by 'It', is out of the game.

This game helps you improve your observation.

Hopscotch

This is one of the oldest games. You can play hopscotch with just one friend. You can also play it by yourself. However, it cannot be played in the grass.

You will need:

- Chalk
- Pebble or shell or any small flat object

Using a chalk, draw the hopscotch pattern as shown.

You can draw the hopscotch pattern in the driveway or on a concrete floor. There are ten squares in the pattern. The first three are vertical squares (1-3). Then there are two horizontal squares (4 and 5). One vertical square (6) is followed by two horizontal squares (7 and 8). There is another vertical square (9) and a final area marked (10).

While drawing the pattern, remember that the square should be large enough for the players to be able to hop on one foot to the other square without touching the lines.

Each player will begin by tossing the marker in the first square. The player will then skip square one and hop on one leg straight to square two and then three.

The player can put both feet down on the horizontal squares 4–5 and 7–8.

When the player reaches square 10, he/she will turn around and start hopping back to the beginning. When the player reaches square 2, he/she will bend down on one leg to pick up the marker from square 1 and then skip over number 1. He/she will now toss the marker in square 2.

The player will have to skip the square in which the marker has been tossed each time.

If the marker is in either square 4 or 5, or in 7 or 8, then the player cannot put both the feet in these squares. He/she will have to hop in each one of them as well. While playing, the marker and your foot should not touch the lines of the pattern.

If a player is unable to toss the marker in the correct box, he/she is out and the next player will take his/her turn. When the second player is out, the first player will start from where he/she had left. A player who has placed a marker in each square before the others is the winner.

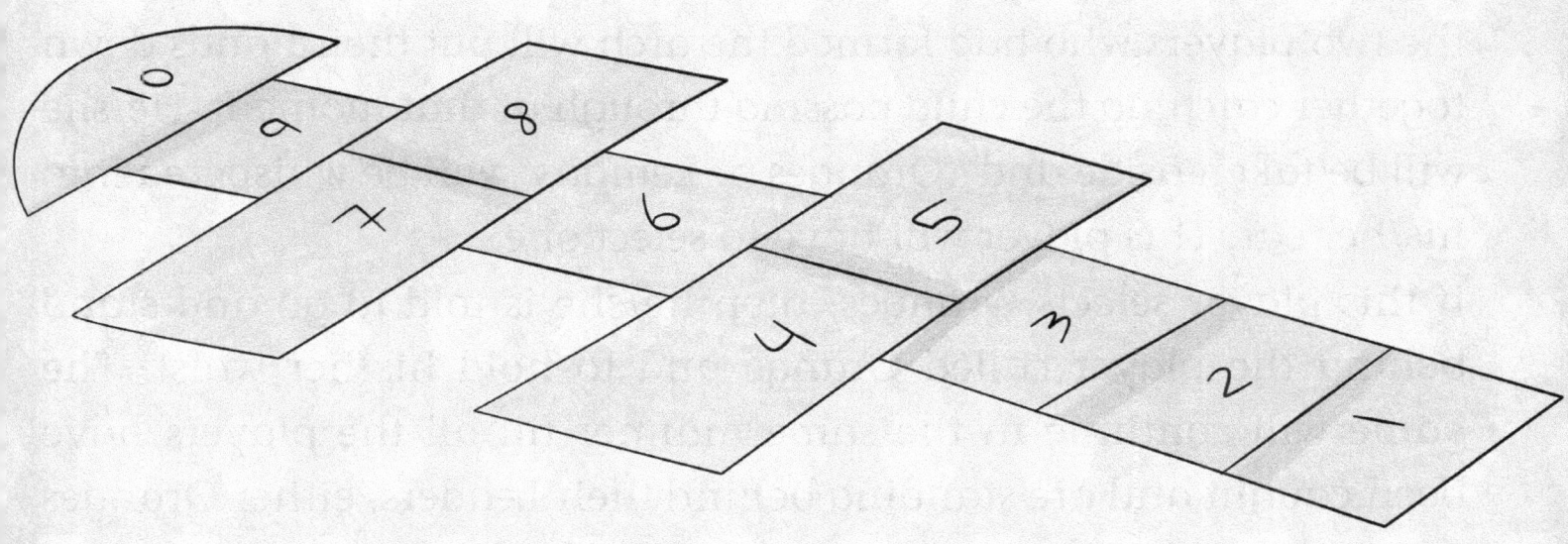

Oranges and Lemons

It is always merrier to play this game with a lot of friends. Two players stand facing each other forming an arch with their arms raised above and fingers joined together. Secretly both the players should decide who would be 'orange' and 'lemon'. Meanwhile, the other players will start singing the song, "oranges and lemon" while running through the arch in a line.

"Oranges and lemon,

Sold for a penny

All the schoolgirls

Are so many

The grass is green

And the rose is red

Remember me when I am dead, dead, dead, dead."

The moment the players come to saying 'dead, dead, dead, dead', the two players who had formed the arch will put their hands down together catching the child passing through at that moment. He/she will be taken aside and "Oranges or Lemons" will be whispered into his/her ear. This player will have to select one.

If this player selects Oranges, then he/she is told to go and stand behind the player called Orange and to hold his/her waist. The game will continue in the same manner till all the players have been caught and are standing behind their Leaders, either Oranges or Lemons.

Now comes the fun part. There will be a tug-of-war between Oranges and Lemons. A line will be drawn between the two teams. Soon, the two teams will begin pulling each other. The team that crosses the line to the other side will lose. The stronger and the most united team will win.

Memory Game

This game will boost your memory. It is also a game where you will need to listen carefully and understand what is being said. There can be as many players as you want to play this game.

Gather yourselves in a circle. One among the players will whisper a small sentence to the player sitting next to him/ her. Let's say player 1 said: 'I went shopping.' The player next to him/her will repeat what player 1 has said and add something more to it. Let's say Player 2 says: 'I went shopping and bought a hat.' Player 3 has to repeat what players 1 and 2 have said and add something more. Let's say Player 3 says: 'I went shopping and bought a hat and boots.'

In this manner this game will go on. When someone forgets to add what had been said before, or is unable to add something, he/she is out of the game. The player who remains when others are out is the winner.

Did you enjoy playing these games?

Be innovative and make your own game by combining one or more of the ones we talked about!

Have a great time playing indoors and outdoors!